A PRAYER A DAY

365 prayers – one for every day of the year

Compiled by Mark Water

Illustrated by Caroline Ewen

STANDARD
PUBLISHING

ISBN 0-7847-0973-4

Published in the United States by
The Standard Publishing Company
8121 Hamilton Ave.Cincinnati, Ohio 45231.
A division of Standex International Corporation.

Original edition published in English under
the title *A Prayer A Day* by Hunt & Thorpe,
Alresford, Hants, UK.

Printed and bound in Malaysia by Times Offset

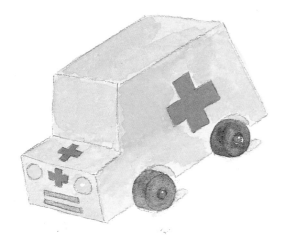

Contents

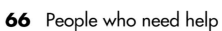

Good morning

1 **THIS NEW DAY**

Thank you, Lord,
for keeping me safe through the past night.
Thank you, Lord,
for this new day.
Amen.

William Canton

2 **AS I PLAY**

Dear Lord Jesus,
thank you for all my toys
and all the games I play.
Please help me to have a happy time
as I play with all my friends today.
Amen.

3 **MORNING LIGHT**

Father God,
for sleep and rest,
for morning light,
and a bright new day, thank you.
Amen.

Henry William Baker

4 **GOOD MORNING**

Good morning, Lord Jesus.
It's great to know your love and friendship
as I start this new day.
Thank you, Lord Jesus, for being my friend.
Amen.

5 THIS NEW MORNING

For this new morning and its light,
For rest and shelter of the night,
For health and food, for love and friends,
For every gift your goodness sends,
We thank you, Lord.
Amen.

6 WAKING UP

As I wake
and see the light,
I know God's kept me
through the night.

William Canton

7 FOR THE START OF THE DAY

Teach me, Lord God,
to do everything
that I do today
as if I am doing it for you.
Amen.

George Herbert

8 A GIFT

May I remember, dear Lord,
that every day
comes as a gift from you,
to be used in a way
that pleases you.
Amen.

Samuel Johnson

9 FATHER LEAD ME

Father God,
take me through this new day.
Make me kind and true
and show me what I ought to do.

John Hobbs

10 FIRST THOUGHTS

Lord Jesus,
– as I wake up,
– as I open my eyes,
– as I stretch and yawn,
– as the new day dawns,
I know you are my Lord,
and you are here.

11 GOD BEFORE ME

God before me,
God behind me,
God above me,
God within me,
this day and every day,
I pray.
Amen.

12 KEEP US SAFE

Heavenly Father,
thank you for bringing us safely
to the beginning of this new day.
Keep us safe by your great power.
Do not let us fall into sin
or run into danger today.
Guide us in all that we do,
and help us to do what is right.
Amen.

The Book of Common Prayer

God's world

1 ALL THINGS BRIGHT AND BEAUTIFUL

Chorus:
All things bright and beautiful,
All creatures great and small,
All things wise and wonderful,
The Lord God made them all.

C.F. Alexander

2 SUNSETS

The purple-headed mountain,
The river running by,
The sunset and the morning
That brightens up the sky.
Chorus

C.F. Alexander

3 WIND AND SUN

The cold wind in the winter,
The pleasant summer sun,
The ripe fruits in the garden,
He made them every one.
Chorus

C.F. Alexander

4 FOR THE BEAUTY OF THE EARTH

For the beauty of the earth,
For the beauty of the skies,
For the love which from our birth
Over and around us lies,
  Christ, our God, to thee we raise
  This our sacrifice of praise.

F.S. Pierpoint

8

5 FOR THE BEAUTY OF EACH HOUR

For the beauty of each hour
Of the day and of the night,
Hill and vale and tree and flower,
Sun and moon and stars of light,
   Christ, our God, to thee we raise
   This our sacrifice of praise.

F.S. Pierpoint

6 IN EVERY PLACE

Lord,
make me see your glory
in every place.
Amen.

Michelangelo

7 ALL CREATURES

All creatures of our God and King
Lift up your voice and with us sing,
   Alleluiah, alleluiah!
You burning sun with golden beam,
You silver moon with softer gleam,
   O praise him, O praise him,
   Alleluiah, alleluiah, alleluiah!

St. Francis of Assisi

8 FLOWING WATER

Fast flowing water, pure and clear,
Make music for your Lord to hear,
   Alleluiah, alleluiah!
Flames of fire, masterful and bright,
You give to us both warmth and light.
   O praise him, O praise him,
   Alleluiah, alleluiah, alleluiah!

St. Francis of Assisi

11 GLORY BE TO GOD

Glory be to God for all the planets,
glory be to God for outer space,
glory be to God for blue skies
   and white clouds,
glory be to you, Lord God, for your creation.

Gerard Manley Hopkins

9 RUSHING RIVERS

Lord God,
you have made such a wonderful world:
bright stars, towering mountains,
rushing rivers,
and deep, deep seas.
We sing your praises
for your wonderful world.

12 OUR UNIVERSE

Dear Father God,
in the sky at night
I can see the moon
   and thousands of stars.
And there are millions
   and millions more stars
   that are so far away
   we can't even see them
   with a telescope.
You made them all.
How great you are!
Amen.

10 RUNNING WATER

Lord God, we thank you for the earth,
   our home:
for the wide sky and shimmering sun,
for the salt sea and running water,
for the everlasting hills
and the endless winds,
for all the trees and all the grass.
Give us hearts wide open to all your beauty.
Amen.

Walter Rauschenbusch

God – our Father

1 LOVING FATHER

We thank you, Father God,
for all your special care.
We thank you, Father God,
for all the clothes we wear.
Amen.

2 GOD MADE THE EARTH

God, who made the earth,
The air, the sky, the sea,
Who gave the light its birth,
You care for me.

S.B. Rhodes

3 GOD MADE THE GRASS

God, who made the grass,
The flower, the fruit, the tree,
The day and night to pass,
You care for me.

S.B. Rhodes

4 GOD MADE THE SUN

God, who made the sun,
The moon, the stars, is he
Who, when life's clouds come on
Who cares for me.

S.B. Rhodes

5 HE IS KIND

Let us thank God with our mind,
Praise the Lord, for he is kind,
Chorus:
> *For his mercies will endure,*
> *Ever faithful, ever sure.*

John Milton

6 LIGHT

Let us thank God for the light,
Praise the Lord, for his great might,
> *Chorus.*

John Milton

7 ALL THINGS

Let us thank God for all things,
Praise the Lord, for what he brings,
> *Chorus.*

John Milton

8 FOR SEAS AND BEES

Let us thank God for the seas,
Praise the Lord, for all the bees.
Chorus.

John Milton

5 I'LL SEE YOU THROUGH

Jesus says,
"If you are tired
from carrying heavy burdens,
come to me
and I will give you rest.
The load with my help is light."

Matthew 11:28-29

6 DO NOT BE AFRAID

Jesus says,
"Don't be afraid!
I am the first, the last,
and the living one.
I am alive for ever."

Revelation 1:17-18

7 I WILL COME IN

Jesus says,
"Here I am!
I stand at the door and knock.
If anyone hears my voice and
    opens
        the door,
I will come in and eat with them
    and
        they with me."

Revelation 3:20

8 HAPPY ARE THOSE ...

Jesus says,
"Happy are those who have not seen me
and yet have believed."

John 20:29

9 FORGIVE

Jesus says,
"Don't be hard on others,
    and God will not be hard
        on you.
Forgive others,
    and God will forgive you.
The way you treat others
    is the way
        you will be treated."

Luke 6:37-38

10 EVERYBODY YOU MEET

Jesus says,
"Treat everybody you meet
in the same way you would
like them to treat you."

Luke 6:31

11 GOD CARES FOR EVERYBODY

Jesus says,
"God is your Father and you must live in his
    way.
He cares for everybody, everywhere –
bad people and good people;
honest people and dishonest people.
See how the sun shines
and the rain falls on all their farms alike."

Matthew 5:45

12 HE WILL MAKE US CLEAN

John, Jesus' friend, says,
"If we own up to our sins,
God will forgive our sins.
We can trust God.
He does what is right.
He will make us clean from
    all the wrongs we have done."

1 John 1:9. International Children's Bible

Thank you

1 ALL THE GIFTS

Lord Jesus,
thank you for all the gifts
you keep on giving us.
Give us one more thing –
a grateful heart. Amen.

George Herbert

2 TOYS

Heavenly Father,
I love playing with all my toys.
Thank you for giving me
   eyes to see them,
   hands to arrange them,
   and imagination to have such fun.
Amen.

3 RAINBOWS

Lord Jesus,
I love rainbows.
Thank you for their stunning colors,
and their lovely shape.
Thank you that they are a sign from you
that you care for and love your world.
Amen.

4 NOW THANK WE ALL OUR GOD

Now thank we all our God,
With hearts and hands and voices,
Great wonders he has done,
In him the world rejoices.
He, from our mother's arms,
Has blessed us on our way
With countless gifts of love
And still is ours today.

M. Rinkhart

5 YOUR LOVE LASTS

Thank you, Lord,
because you are good.
Your love lasts for ever.
Amen.

Psalm 107:1

6 FOR RAIN AND PUDDLES

Dear Lord God,
    For rain and puddles,
        we thank you.
    For flowers and blackberries in hedges,
        we thank you.
    For ladybirds,
        we thank you.
    For snowflakes and snowballs,
        we thank you.
Amen.

7 COOKING

Cooking:
Mix a pancake.
Stir a pancake
Pour it in the pan.
Fry the pancake.
Toss the pancake.
Catch it if you can!
Thank you, Lord Jesus,
for all the fun I have
trying to cook.
Amen.

Christina Rossetti

8 ALL THINGS

Thank you, Lord Jesus,
for giving us so many things
to enjoy each day.

1 Timothy 6:17

9 TELEVISION

Dear Lord Jesus,
I love to watch TV:
    – the stories,
    – the cartoons
    – the songs.
Thank you for all the people
who make the programs.
Amen.

10 MODERN INVENTIONS

Heavenly Father,
thank you for modern inventions:
    – for computers,
    – for spaceships,
    – for new medicines.
May they be used wisely
to help everyone.
Amen.

11 MY CLOTHES

Dear Lord Jesus,
how I love my clothes:
    – their colors,
    – their styles,
    – the way they feel.
Thank you for all my clothes,
and my shoes.
Amen.

12 BOOKS

Thank you, Lord Jesus, for books:
    – for their pictures,
    – for their stories,
    – for their poems,
    – for science books,
    – for nature books,
    – for information books.
And thank you for your book,
    the Bible,
    where I learn about you.
Amen.

Mealtimes

1 THE FOOD WE EAT

Thank you for the world so sweet.
Thank you for the food we eat.
Thank you for the birds that sing.
Thank you, God, for everything.

E. Rutter Leatham

2 OUR GUEST

Come, Lord Jesus, be our guest,
And may our meal by you be blessed.
Amen.

3 BLESS THIS FOOD

Bless, O Lord, this food to our use
and ourselves in your service,
through Jesus Christ our Lord.
Amen.

4 DAILY FOOD

For health and strength and daily food,
We praise your name, our Lord.
Amen.

5 FOOD FOR STRENGTH

Bless me, dear Lord Jesus,
and let my food
strengthen me to serve you.
Amen.

Isaac Watts

6 THANK YOU

For every cup and plateful,
Lord, make us truly grateful.
Amen.

Author not known

7 ALL LIVING THINGS

Let us thank God who does feed
all living creatures in their need.
For his mercies will endure,
ever faithful, ever sure.

John Milton

8 DIFFERENT TASTES

Lord Jesus, we thank you
for so many different tastes:
   – for spicy chicken,
   – for smooth, sweet chocolate,
   – for salty potato chips,
   – and for tart, juicy lemons.

9 DRINKS

For ice cool summer drinks
to refresh us,
for warming winter drinks
to strengthen us,
thank you, Lord.

10 DAILY BREAD

Dear Lord Jesus,
we now say a big
"thank you" to you
for our daily bread,
and those clear, cool glasses
of drinking water.

11 THANKFUL HEARTS

We thank you, then, our Father
for all things bright and good;
the seed-time and the harvest,
our life, our health, our food.
Accept the gifts we offer
for all your love imparts;
and that which you most welcome,
our humble, thankful hearts.

M. Claudius

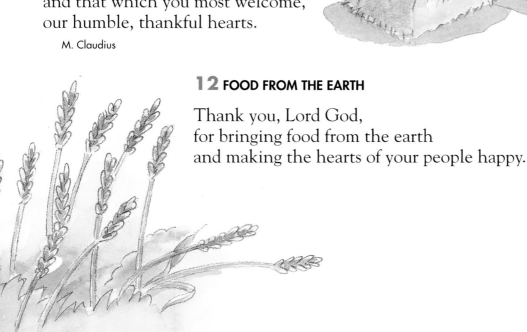

12 FOOD FROM THE EARTH

Thank you, Lord God,
for bringing food from the earth
and making the hearts of your people happy.

My family, friends, and home

1 MY HOME

Dear heavenly Father,
thank you for my home and family.
Please may your love be always with us,
Please may your care always protect us,
Please may your peace always surround us.
Amen.

2 THANK YOU

Dear heavenly Father,
thank you especially for _____
(*add the name of a special person*)
who always loves me,
who always has time to listen to me,
and play with me,
who always wants to help me,
and understands when I'm sad.
Amen.

3 MY FRIEND

Thank you for my friend next door,
And my friend across the street.
Lord, please help me to be a friend
To everyone I meet.
Amen.

Author not known

4 VISIT US, LORD

Visit we pray, Lord Jesus,
  our home
  and keep us safe from all attacks
  of the evil one.
May your presence rest on us
  and keep us in your peace,
  and your blessing always stay with us.
Amen.

5 MY RELATIVES

Thank you for my relatives, Lord Jesus.
  Please take care of them. I pray for _____.
Amen.

6 FEELING SAFE

Dear Lord Jesus,
thank you for _____,
who always makes me feel safe.
Amen.

7 MY FAMILY

Thank you, Lord Jesus,
for all my family.
Thank you for the family
I live with each day.
Thank you for the family
we visit and see at Christmas time.
Thank you for all their love.
Amen.

8 ALL WHO OBEY

Thank you, Lord Jesus, that all those who
  obey you are your brothers and sisters.
Amen.

9 I AM SORRY

Dear Lord Jesus,
I am sorry that I've not always
    been kind to my friends.
I am sorry that I've not always
    been happy with my friends.
I am sorry that I've not always
    apologized to my friends.
Amen.

10 MY ROOM

Thank you, Lord Jesus,
    for my room,
    my bed,
    and for the window I look through.
Thank you for being with me
    in my room.
Amen.

11 MOM AND DAD

Dear heavenly Father,
sometimes my Mom and Dad are so busy.
They have so much to do.
Please help them.
Amen.

12 I GOT SO ANGRY

Dear Lord,
I got so angry with _____.
I wanted to shout and scream.
I wanted to kick.
Help _____ to listen to me,
And to understand how I feel.
And help me to understand
how _____ feels.
Amen.

School

1 A SCHOOL DAY

As I go to school today,
Lord Jesus,
help me to trust you
and do everything with all my heart.
Amen.

2 WHEN I DON'T WANT TO GO TO SCHOOL

Dear heavenly Father,
sometimes I don't want to go to school.
I don't want to leave my Mom, my toys,
  and my pet.
Thank you for saying,
"I will never leave you."
Please help me at school.
Amen.

Hebrews 13:5

3 WHEN I GO TO SCHOOL

When I wake up in the morning,
  thank you, Jesus, for being there.
When I go to school each day,
  thank you, Jesus, for being there.
When I'm playing with my friends,
  thank you, Jesus, for being there.
Amen.

4 STRENGTH

I have so much to get through
  today, Lord Jesus.
Please help me to do everything
  in the strength you give me.
Amen.

5 IF I FORGET YOU

Lord, you know how busy
I will be today.
If I forget you,
Please do not forget me.
Amen.

6 TO BE A FRIEND

Lord Jesus,
there's someone at school
    that no one likes.
_____ is always alone.
Children tell stories about _____
Help me to like her/him.
Help me to be a friend.
Amen.

7 WHEN SCHOOL IS FUN

Heavenly Father,
often it's fun at school.
It's fun:
    – finding out about new things,
    – doing experiments,
    – singing,
    – learning math and reading,
    – playing games,
    – painting and making models,
    – hearing stories.
Thank you for school.
Amen.

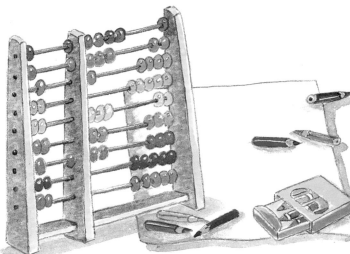

8 WHEN LESSONS ARE HARD

When my lessons are hard
and I don't understand the teacher,
please help me, Lord Jesus.
Please be my guide and teacher as I learn.
Amen.

9 THE MASTER OF MY MIND

Lord and Savior, true and kind,
Be the Master of my mind.
Bless and guide and strengthen still
All my powers of thought and will.
Amen.

H.C.G. Moule

11 WHEN I'M LONELY

Sometimes I'm lonely at school.
The other children leave me out of their
  teams.
Help me to remember that you are my best
  friend.
You are with me in the playground.
You are sitting next to me at my desk.
Amen.

10 MY MEMORY

Lord Jesus, please help me
with all the tests and exams I have,
especially when I'm upset or
worried about them.
Please help me to enjoy all my work
and please give me a good memory.
Amen.

12 STANDING UP FOR JESUS

Dear Lord Jesus,
Help me to stand up for you at school.
Help me not to let you down by anything
  I say or do.
Help me not to be ashamed of praying to you
  and going to church.
Amen.

Animals and birds

1 YOU MADE OUR EARTH

Father God,
You made our earth as a home for:
  – animals,
  – birds,
  – reptiles,
  – insects,
  – fish,
  – as well as for people.
And you told us to take care of the animals.
Please be with all farmers, scientists, vets,
  zoo-keepers, and circus trainers.
Help everybody to be kind to animals,
  and treat them well.
Amen.

2 COWS

Creator God,
we thank you for the mooing,
slow-moving, staring cows.
Thank you for all the milk,
and butter, and cream they give us.
Amen.

3 GOD SEES

God sees the little sparrow fall,
It meets his tender view.
If God so loves the little birds;
I know he loves me too.

Maria Straub 1838–1898

4 THE BUSY ANT

The tiny, busy ant
works like crazy.
Like the ant, help me
to be never lazy.

Based on Proverbs 6:6–8

5 THANK YOU

Lord God,
sometimes in the Bible animals were
      your servants.
   The big fish rescued Jonah.
   Balaam's donkey saw an angel
      and spoke to his master.
   Jesus rode a donkey into Jerusalem.
Thank you for all the animals who
      help us,
      protect us,
      and love us.
Thank you for
      sheep dogs,
      guide dogs,
      horses,
      donkeys,
      and elephants.
     Amen.

6 A PEACEFUL FUTURE

Dear Lord Jesus, thank you that one day,
the wolf and the lamb will feed together,
and the lion will eat straw like the ox.
Amen.

Based on Isaiah 65:25

7 MY PET

Dear Jesus,
I just love my pet!
My pet is always there
   for me.
My pet is always fun and
   full of life.
Thank you, Lord Jesus.
Amen.

8 THE PARK

Thank you, Lord Jesus, for the park:
   – for the trees and flowers,
   – and the long grassy slopes.
But most of all,
   thank you for the ducks on the lake.
Amen.

9 EACH LITTLE FLOWER

Each little flower that opens,
Each little bird that sings,
He made their glowing colors,
He made their tiny wings.

C.F. Alexander

10 GOD IS GREAT

I praise you, Lord,
you are very great.
You make springs flow down the
    mountainsides.
They give water to all the animals.

Psalm 104:1,10

11 BY THE WATER

The wild donkeys come there to drink.
Wild birds make nests by the water.
They sing among the tree branches.
You make the grass for the cattle.

Psalm 104:11-12, International Children's Bible

12 THE STORK'S HOME

The stork's home is in the fir trees.
The high mountains belong to the goats.
The rocks are hiding places for badgers.
You make it dark, and it becomes night.
Then all the wild animals creep around.
All things depend on you.

Psalm 104:17-8,27, International Children's Bible

Christmas

1 AWAY IN A MANGER

Away in a manger, no crib for a bed,
The little Lord Jesus laid down his sweet head;
The stars in the bright sky looked down where he lay,
The little Lord Jesus asleep on the hay.

Martin Luther

2 THE BABY AWAKES

The cattle are lowing, the baby awakes;
But little Lord Jesus, no crying he makes.
I love you, Lord Jesus. Look down from
   the sky,
And stay by my side until morning is nigh.

Martin Luther

3 BE NEAR ME

Be near me, Lord Jesus, I ask you to stay,
Close by me forever, and love me, I pray;
Bless all the dear children in your tender
   care,
And fit us for heaven to live with you there.

Martin Luther

4 COME TO MY HEART, LORD JESUS

You did leave your throne and your kingly
   crown,
When you came to earth for me:
But in Bethlehem's home there was found
   no room
For your holy nativity.
O come to my heart, Lord Jesus.
There is room in my heart for you.

E.E.S. Elliot

5 WHAT CAN I GIVE?

What can I give you,
   Poor as I am?
If I were a shepherd,
   I would bring a lamb.
If I were a wise man,
   I would do my part.
Yet what I can I give you –
   I can give my heart.

Christina Rossetti

6 STAY WITH US

O holy child of Bethlehem,
   Come down to us we pray.
Cast out our sin and enter in,
   Be born in us today.
We hear the Christmas angels
   The great glad tidings tell,
O come to us, abide with us,
   Our Lord Immanuel.

Phillip Brooks

7 LOVE

Love came down at Christmas.
Love all lovely, love divine.
Love was born at Christmas,
Star and angels gave the sign.

Christina Rossetti

8 JOY AND PEACE

May the joy of the angels,
And the peace of the Lord Jesus,
Fill our hearts
At this Christmas time.
Amen.

10 DAVID'S CITY

Once in royal David's city
   Stood a lowly cattle shed,
Where a mother laid her baby
   In a manger for his bed.
Mary was that mother mild,
   Jesus Christ her little child.

C.F. Alexander

11 GOOD AS HE

And through all his wondrous childhood
   He would honor and obey,
Love and watch the gentle mother,
   In whose caring arms he lay.
Christian children all should be
   Kind, obedient, and good as he.

C.F. Alexander

12 LIKE US HE GREW

For he is our childhood's pattern,
   Day by day like us he grew.
He was little, weak and helpless,
   Tears and smiles like us he knew.
And he feels for all our sadness,
   And he shares in all our gladness.

C.F. Alexander

9 A BABY IN BETHLEHEM

Dear Lord Jesus,
how wonderful that you were born as a baby
   in Bethlehem.
How wonderful that you grew up as a boy in
   Nazareth.
Thank you for being like one of us.
Thank you that you know all about falling
   over and tears.
Thank you that you know all about happy
   days and laughing.
Thank you that we can talk to you about
   everything.
Thank you that you understand everything.
Amen.

13 THE WISE

The wise may bring their learning,
　the rich may bring their wealth,
and some may bring their greatness,
　and some their strength and health.
We too would bring our treasures
　to offer to the king.
How shall we greet our Savior,
　what present shall we bring?

14 PLEASE HIM

We'll bring the many duties
　we have to do each day.
We'll try our best to please him,
　at home, at school, at play.
And better are these treasures
　to offer to the king,
than richest gifts without love –
　which we must always bring.

15 HEARTS THAT LOVE HIM

We'll bring him hearts that love him,
　we'll bring him songs of praise,
and lives which keep on trying
　to follow in his ways.
And these will be the treasures
　we offer to the king,
the gifts which now and always
　our grateful hearts may bring.

16 A BABY BOY

The virgin Mary had a baby boy,
The virgin Mary had a baby boy,
The virgin Mary had a baby boy,
And they say that his name is Jesus.

Chorus:
  He come from the glory,
  He come from the glorious kingdom.
  He come from the glory,
  He come from the glorious kingdom.
  O yes, believer!
  O yes, believer!
  He come from the glory,
  He come from the glorious kingdom.

West Indian carol

17 THE ANGELS SANG

The angels sang when the baby was born,
The angels sang when the baby was born,
The angels sang when the baby was born,
And proclaimed him the Savior Jesus.
  Chorus.

West Indian carol

18 THE WISE MEN SAW

The wise men saw where the baby was born,
The wise men saw where the baby was born,
The wise men saw where the baby was born,
And they say that his name was Jesus.
  Chorus.

West Indian carol

Jesus

1 THE JESUS STORY

Dear Lord Jesus,
I love hearing about
all you said and all you did.
Thank you for my Bible
and my teachers at church.
Amen.

2 MANY WONDERFUL THINGS

Lord Jesus, thank you for
the many wonderful things you did
during your life on earth:
– giving food to thousands
   of hungry people,
– healing a twelve-year-old sick girl,
– teaching people
   to love each other.

3 JESUS WITH THE CHILDREN

Dear Lord Jesus,
I am so happy to know
that you took children
into your arms,
showed your love for them,
and blessed them
when you met them.
Please be with me
all through this day.
Amen.

4 JESUS AND HIS MIRACLES

Lord Jesus,
Thank you
for all your miracles,
like when the wind and the waves
were about to drown
your followers in their boat
and you calmed the sea.
Help me to trust you
whenever I am in danger.
Amen.

5 MY BEST FRIEND

Dear Lord Jesus,
   thank you
   that you are my best friend.
Thank you,
   that you never stop loving me.
Amen.

6 WITH ALL MY HEART

Dear Lord Jesus,
  I love you with all my heart.
Thank you for loving me
  with all your heart.
Amen.

7 FRIEND OF LITTLE CHILDREN

Jesus, friend of little children,
  Be a friend to me.
Take my hand and always keep me
  Close to you.

W.J. Mathams

8 FEARS AND WORRIES

Dear Lord Jesus,
please help me, when I am afraid,
and when I lie in bed at night,
full of worries.
Amen.

9 WHAT A FRIEND

What a friend we have in Jesus,
All our sins and griefs to bear.
What a privilege to carry
Everything to God in prayer.

J.M. Scriven

10 JESUS KNOWS

Dear Lord Jesus,
You share all our sorrows,
and you know all our weaknesses.
Please comfort and strengthen us.
Amen.

11 YOU LOVED

Dear Jesus,
You loved sparrows and wild flowers,
You loved your friends,
You helped people who were:
  – lonely,
  – poor,
  – afraid,
  – and ill.
Sometimes you were lonely and cold,
  sad and hungry.
In your stories you told us that
  our Father God cares for us all.
Thank you, Lord Jesus.
Amen.

12 NOT ASHAMED

Lord Jesus,
  you were poor,
  you were unknown,
  you were laughed at.
Help me not to be ashamed
  to follow you.
Amen.

John Wesley

Easter

1 PALM SUNDAY

Dear Lord Jesus,
thank you for being humble enough
to ride into Jerusalem,
not on a grand horse,
but on a common donkey.
Please may I
follow your example
and be humble in my heart
and humble in all I do.
Amen.

2 GOOD FRIDAY

There is a green hill far away
   Outside a city wall,
Where our dear Lord was crucified,
   Who died to save us all.

C.F. Alexander

3 NO OTHER GOOD ENOUGH

There was no other good enough
   To pay the price of sin.
He only could unlock the gate
   Of heaven and let us in.

C.F. Alexander

4 YOU LOVED SO MUCH

Lord Jesus,
you loved us so much
that you died for us.
Help us, in return,
to love you so much
that we live for you.
Amen.

5 MOST WONDERFUL

It is a thing most wonderful,
    Almost too wonderful to be,
That God's own Son should come
        from heaven,
    And die to save a child like me.

W.W. How

6 IT IS TRUE

And yet I know that it is true,
    He came to this poor world below,
And wept, and toiled, and mourned,
        and died,
    Only because he loved us so.

W.W. How

7 WONDERFUL LOVE

It is most wonderful to know
    His love for me so free and sure.
His love must be most wonderful,
    If he could die, my love to win.

W.W. How

8 I WANT TO LOVE YOU

And yet I want to love you, Lord,
    Help me to grow and grow in grace,
That I may love you more and more,
    Until I'm with you, face to face.

W.W. How

9 ON EASTER SUNDAY

Dear Lord Jesus,
I am so happy because
    you did not stay dead.
On Easter Sunday
    you came alive again.
And you are alive today
    and forever.
Amen.

10 JESUS IS ALIVE

Jesus Christ is risen today, Alleluia,
Our triumphant holy day, Alleluia,
Who did once upon the cross, Alleluia,
Suffer to redeem our loss, Alleluia.

11 RISEN FROM THE DEAD

He is Lord,
He is Lord,
He is risen from the dead,
And he is Lord!
Every knee will bow,
Every tongue will say
That Jesus Christ is Lord.

12 EASTER

Thank you, Lord Jesus,
    for Easter
    – for Easter eggs,
    and for Easter holidays.
but most of all,
    thank you for being alive forever
    and with us every day.
Amen.

God's Word and God's Spirit

1 THANK YOU FOR THE BIBLE

Dear Father God,
thank you for the Bible.
Thank you for its stories, its poems,
    and songs.
Thank you that it teaches us about you.
Amen.

2 READ, NOTE, LEARN

Dear Lord,
you inspired all the Bible
    to be written for us to read.
Each time we come to the Bible
    help us to:
    – listen to your voice,
    – read,
    – note,
    – learn,
    – and take your message
    to our hearts,
so that we may love you
    as our Savior.
Amen.

The Book of Common Prayer

3 JESUS LOVES ME

Jesus loves me, this I know,
For the Bible tells me so.
Little ones to him belong,
They are weak but he is strong.

Anna Warner

4 TRANSLATORS

Thank you, Lord Jesus, for all the people
who have translated the Bible into English
and into other languages. Please help
Bible translators and Bible teachers today.
Help them to be patient. Give them
understanding to choose the right words.
Amen.

5 NO BIBLES

In some countries no one is allowed to
buy or sell the Bible. If people can get a Bible,
they read it secretly. Please help these people,
dear Lord. Help them to be brave.
Keep them safe. Help people who
want Bibles to get hold of copies.
Amen.

6 A LAMP

Thank you, Father,
that the Bible is like a lamp
to my feet,
and a light
to my path.
It shows me how
I ought to live.
Amen.

Psalm 119

7 AS I READ THE BIBLE

Dear Lord, open my eyes
that I may see
the wonderful truths
in the pages of the Bible.
Amen.

Psalm 119:18

8 THE SPIRIT OF JESUS

Dear Lord Jesus, I'm so glad
your Holy Spirit is with me.
Help me to live in such a way
that I never make you sad.
Amen.

9 HERE ALL THE TIME

Dear heavenly Father,
when Jesus went to heaven,
you sent your Holy Spirit
to be with us.
Your Spirit is the same
as Jesus being with us.
Thank you that your Spirit
is here to help us
all the time.
Amen.

10 HOLY SPIRIT

Holy Spirit, hear me
When I kneel to pray.
Come to me and teach me
What I ought to say.

From a hymn by W.H. Parker

11 RULE OUR HEARTS

Lord God,
Without you
We are not able to please you,
Please may your Holy Spirit
Guide us in everything we do
And be in charge of our hearts.
Amen.

The Book of Common Prayer

12 HE WILL GUIDE US

Christ is the first and the last,
    His Spirit will guide us safely home.
We'll praise him for all that is past,
    And trust him for all that's to come.

J. Hort

I'm sorry

1 TEACH ME

Teach me to do the thing that's right,
    And when I'm wrong, forgive.
And make me willing day and night,
    To serve you while I live.

Jane Taylor

2 UNKIND WORDS

Heavenly Father, I know you hate it
when I say unkind words,
when I do unkind things,
and when I think unkind thoughts.
Please help me to be kind today.
Amen.

3 BAD TEMPER

Dear Father God,
I got very angry today,
and then I sulked. I'm sorry.
Amen.

4 FORGIVE ME, LORD

Forgive me, Lord Jesus,
for any wrong thoughts I had,
for any unkind words I said,
and any bad things I did today.
Amen.

5 WE ARE SORRY

We are sorry that we have done what we
 should not have done.
We are sorry that we have not done what
 we should have done.
Please forgive us.
Help us to live to please you tomorrow.
Amen.

6 PLEASE FORGIVE

We are sorry, Lord Jesus,
for the naughty things
we have done today.
Please forgive us,
and help us,
Lord Jesus,
to please you tomorrow.
Amen.

7 TO START AGAIN

Dear Father God,
thank you for your great love.
When I do wrong things,
and am sorry – you forgive me.
You forget all about the wrong things
and you help me to start again.
Amen.

8 WHEN I'M GREEDY

Dear Jesus,
sometimes I'm greedy.
I want too much
and I grab things for myself.
I'm sorry.
Please help me to share
and to give
and to think of others.
Amen.

9 NO CLOUDS

Dear heavenly Father, thank you for forgiving me the wrong things I have done, when I am really sorry. I sometimes feel that the bad things I do are like big clouds between you and me. Thank you for sweeping away these clouds so I feel the warmth of your love, like sunshine. Amen.

10 A FRIEND SO FAITHFUL

Can we find a friend so faithful
    Who will all our sorrows share?
Jesus knows our every weakness
    Take it to the Lord in prayer.

J. Scriven

11 TRUSTING IN JESUS

Dear Lord Jesus,
    thank you for loving
    me so much.
Thank you for forgiving me
    when I say "I'm sorry" to you.
You are my best Friend.
Amen.

12 I'M SORRY

Dear Lord Jesus,
I'm sorry that I
don't always want
to apologize.
Please help me
to be as loving,
and forgiving
as you are.
Amen.

Please help

1 HELP US

Loving Father, help us
    Each day with your might,
To turn away from wrong,
    And choose what is right.

W.H. Parker

2 ALL NIGHT LONG

Dear Father God,
The nights are so dark.
There are shadows,
and noises I don't understand.
Thank you that you are
looking after me all night long.
Amen.

3 READING THE BIBLE

When I listen to Bible stories, dear Lord,
help me to understand what
you are saying to me.
Help me to enjoy
hearing and reading the Bible.
Amen.

4 WHEN WE ARE SAD

Please give us, Lord Jesus:
– in all our difficulties, your help;
– in all our dangers, your protection;
– and in all our sad times, your comfort.
Amen.

St. Augustine

5 DOGS

Dear Lord Jesus,
sometimes I get scared of dogs.
Little dogs are so bouncy and yappy.
Big dogs are so tall.
Their barks are so loud.
They growl.
They have sharp teeth.
But I know you are with me.
When I see a dog,
help me to stop being frightened.
Amen.

6 PEOPLE

There are some people, Lord Jesus,
I don't like very much.
I don't feel happy
when I'm with them.
But you love them.
Please may they know your love.
Please help them.
Amen.

7 POWER

I get up today with,
– the power of God to guide me,
– the wisdom of God to teach me,
– the eye of God to watch over me,
– the hand of God to protect me,
– and the shield of God to shelter me.
Amen.

8 MAKE US LIKE JESUS

Father God, you have made us.
Lord Jesus, you have forgiven us.
Please help us to be more like you
    in our thinking,
    and in everything we do.
Amen.

9 STORMS

Dear Lord Jesus,
storms can be scary.
The thunder is so loud.
The lightning is so bright.
But thunder and lightning are
    beautiful, too.
Your friends were scared
in a storm at sea,
but you kept them safe.
Please keep me and my family
safe in storms.
Amen.

10 A FAITHFUL FRIEND

Thank you, Lord Jesus,
for sharing my sadness.
Thank you, Lord Jesus,
that you know all about me.
Amen.

11 A HARD DAY

Dear Lord Jesus,
today will be a hard day
because _____
Be with me in all my speaking today.
Be with me in all my thinking today.
Be with me in all I do today.
Amen.

12 JESUS IS LISTENING

Lord Jesus,
Thank you for always hearing my prayers,
Even when they are quick and short.
Thank you for hearing me,
Especially when I am sad.
Amen.

Living like Jesus

1 MORE LIKE JESUS

Dear Lord Jesus,
as I grow taller,
run faster,
and jump higher,
make me grow more like you.
Amen.

2 JESUS' HANDS WERE KIND HANDS

Jesus' hands were kind hands,
  doing good to all.
Healing pain and sickness,
  blessing children small.
Washing tired feet,
  and saving those who fall.
Jesus' hands were kind hands,
  doing good to all.

M. Cropper

3 TAKE MY HANDS

Take my hands, Lord Jesus,
  Let them work for you.
Make them strong and gentle,
  kind in all I do.
Let me watch you, Jesus,
  till I'm gentle too.
Till my hands are kind hands,
  quick to work for you.

M. Cropper

4 LORD OF THE LOVING HEART

Lord of the loving heart,
  May mine be loving too.
Lord of the gentle hands,
  May mine be gentle too.
Lord of the willing feet,
  May mine be willing too.
So may I grow more like you
  In all I say and do.
Amen.

5 FAITH, HOPE, LOVE

Give me, good Lord,
complete faith,
strong hope,
and lots of love.
Amen.

Thomas More

6 THE GIFT OF LOVE

Dear Lord,
you have told us
that everything we do
is no good
unless it is done in love.
With the Spirit of Jesus
in our lives and hearts,
give us this most wonderful gift of love.
Amen.

The Book of Common Prayer

7 JUDGING OTHER PEOPLE

Dear Lord Jesus,
help me not to think bad thoughts
about my friends.
They may have problems
that I don't know about.
Amen.

8 LOVE IS

Love is patient –
Lord Jesus, make me patient.
Love is kind –
Lord Jesus, make me kind.
Love is not proud –
Lord Jesus, make me humble.
Lord Jesus, make me like you.
Amen.

9 SING HOSANNA

Sing hosanna, sing hosanna,
Sing hosanna to the King of kings;
Sing hosanna, sing hosanna,
Sing hosanna to the King.

10 PEACE IN MY HEART

Give me peace in my heart, keep me resting.
Give me peace in my heart, I pray.
Give me peace in my heart, keep me resting.
Keep me resting to the break of day.

11 LOVE FOR EVERYONE

Dear Lord Jesus,
Please may I have your love in my heart today:
– your love for everyone I speak to,
– your love even for the people I don't like.
– and most of all, may I have love for you.
Amen.

12 LOVE TO KEEP US CLOSE

May the Lord Jesus give us light
    to guide us.
May the Lord Jesus give us courage
    to support us.
May the Lord Jesus give us love
    to keep us close together.
Amen.

Dancing and singing days

1 GOD LOVES ME

Dear loving Father,
I am so happy to know
That you love me so much,
And that, to me, you are like
The best father in the world.
Amen.

2 PLAYING

I've been playing
with my best friend today,
and we've had such a great time.
Thank you, Lord Jesus.
Amen.

3 MY PET

Dear Lord Jesus,
thank you for my pet, _____
Thank you for all the hours
we spend together,
and for all the joy _____
brings to me.
Amen.
(*Say your pet's name in the blanks.*)

4 OUR VACATION

Tomorrow is our vacation!
Three cheers – hurray!
　Hurray!
　Hurray!
I'm so excited – I can't sit still.
I'm so happy – I'm nearly ill!
Dear Lord Jesus, I've come to say,
Take care of us on our vacation.
Amen.

5 UP IN A SWING

How I love feeling the air
　　rushing by my face.
Lord Jesus, as I swing into the air,
I love seeing the blue sky roll past
as I go higher and higher,
I'm glad to be going so fast.

6 SO HAPPY

I trust in your love.
My heart is happy because you saved me.
I sing to the Lord
　　because he has taken care of me.

Psalm 13:5,6, International Children's Bible

7 EACH SUNDAY

Thank you,
Lord Jesus,
for our Sundays.
They are always such great days.
Thank you for the church
I go to in the mornings
and for all the friends I meet there.
Thank you that I am at home
in the evenings
with my family.
Amen.

8 HAPPY DAYS

For all the things
that make me happy:
– for adventures in the wind and rain,
– for going head-over-heels on the grass,
dear Lord Jesus, thank you.
Amen.

9 BEING HAPPY WITH JESUS

Dear Lord Jesus,
Just being with you,
Makes me most wonderfully happy.
Thank you
That I can talk to you in prayer,
At any time in the day,
And whenever I wake up at night.
Amen.

11 THIS IS THE DAY

This is the day,
    that the Lord has made.
Let us rejoice, and be glad today!

Psalm 118:24, International Children's Bible

10 HAPPY BIRTHDAY

Happy birthday to you.
    Happy birthday to you.
Happy birthday dear _____
    God bless you today.

12 GOOD NEWS

Dear Lord Jesus,
I want to laugh and dance and sing.
I want to jump and twirl and spring
Up into the air – and right down.
I want to grin and act the clown.
I want to come to you and pray,
With all my heart I want to say
THANK YOU for the news –
The good news we've heard today.
Amen.

Tough and rough days

1 CLOUDY DAYS

Dear heavenly Father,
some of my days are like
thick, dark, heavy clouds,
and I feel down and fed up.
Please help me through my cloudy days.
Amen.

2 GOING TO JESUS

When things are tough at school,
    help me to trust you,
        Lord Jesus.
When everything goes wrong,
    help me to trust you,
        Lord Jesus.
When I feel very, very sad,
    help me to trust you,
        Lord Jesus.
Amen.

3 MY WORK

Dear Lord Jesus,
sometimes my work at school
seems so hard to do.
Help me to do my best
and trust you,
even when I can't do everything.
Amen.

4 WHEN I AM AFRAID

Even when I go through
the worst difficulties,
I will not be afraid, Lord Jesus,
for you are with me.

Psalm 23:4

5 A FATHER'S LOVE

Dear heavenly Father,
When I feel:
   – upset with my friends,
   – or angry with everyone,
   – or really bad-tempered,
May I then remember
   your great love for me.
Amen.

6 MY PET HAS DIED

Dear Lord Jesus,
my pet has died.
You know how much
I loved him/her.
Thank you for his/her life
and all the loving days
and happy times
we had together.
Amen.

7 WHEN TEMPTATION COMES

I keep on giving in
to my temper
and doing wrong things!
May I do better tomorrow,
Lord Jesus.
Amen.

8 WHEN I'M ILL

When I'm ill in bed
and feeling very weak,
I know that your special care
is with me, Lord Jesus.
In my illness may I feel your love.
Amen.

9 I'M FED UP

Dear Lord Jesus,
everything seems to be going
wrong today.
I feel so fed up.
Help me to think about you,
and about your love,
and to be happy again.
Amen.

10 AWAY FROM HOME

I am here away from home,
Lord Jesus, help me.
I am here in need,
Lord Jesus, help me.
I am here in pain,
Lord Jesus, help me.
I am here in trouble,
Lord Jesus, help me.
I am here alone,
Lord Jesus, help me.
Amen.

11 IT'S NOT FAIR

Dear Lord Jesus,
   things seem so unfair!
Sometimes I feel as if
   I never get what I want,
   but everybody else does.
Help me not to mind.
Help me to remember that
   you love me
   and give me all I need
   when I feel like this.
Amen.

12 YOU HELD HER HAND

Dear Lord Jesus,
when a young girl was very ill
   you went to her,
   held her hand
   and made her well again.
Dear Lord Jesus,
I feel so sick today –
   please make me well again.
Thank you for being with me.
Thank you for loving me.
Amen.

The Church – friends of God

1 GOD'S FAMILY

Thank you, dear heavenly Father,
that everyone who loves you
belongs to your family – the Church.
Amen.

2 FRIENDS AT CHURCH

Dear Lord Jesus,
thank you for all the friends
you have given me at church.
May we grow to love you more
and to love each other better.
Amen.

3 TOGETHER

Dear Father God,
there are so many different churches,
    and so many different ways of showing
        love to you.
Help the people in your churches
    to pray together,
    and work together,
    and show your love all the time.
Amen.

4 THE WORLD

Dear Lord Jesus,
it's so great
    that your followers are everywhere:
    – in sleepy villages
    – in busy towns
    – and in tall skyscrapers.
Please give your strength
    to your followers
    who feel lonely.
Amen.

5 STAND UP FOR JESUS

Dear Lord Jesus,
I pray now for your followers
    who are made fun of,
    who are not allowed to:
    – go to church
    – read their Bibles
    – teach children about you.
May they know that you
    are especially close to them.

6 AWAKE

We thank you, heavenly Father,
that your followers are all over the world
in places like Australia, America, China,
    India, Russia, France, Germany
    and Great Britain.
Thank you that when we sleep
    there is somebody awake
    singing your praises.

7 JOY

Dear Father God,
    it's so wonderful to be alive
    and to have your joy in our lives.

8 LEADERS

Dear Father God,
    please be with
    all preachers, and ministers,
    and all Sunday school teachers
    as they teach us each week.
Help all people who:
    – sing in church choirs,
    – hand out song books,
    – read the Bible out aloud,
    – and tell us stories about Jesus.
Help them to be wise and loving
    in their work for you.
Amen.

9 SUNDAY SCHOOL

Thank you, Lord Jesus, for my
Sunday school and youth group, and for all
the times when we learn about you.
Amen.

10 SINGING

Dear Lord Jesus, thank you
that I can sing
songs and choruses,
to show how much I love you.
Amen.

11 HELPING

Dear Lord Jesus,
when I am asked to help
at school or at church,
may I do it as if
I'm doing it for you.
Amen.

12 PRAYING

Dear heavenly Father,
I'm so happy
that I can talk to you anywhere
  in prayer
– at home, in school,
or walking along the road.
Amen.

All over the world

1 PEACE TO OTHERS

Lord God, help me to spread a little happiness
    to all the people I meet today.
Help me to spread a little of your love
    to all the people I meet today.
Help me to spread a little peace
    to all the people I meet today.
Amen.

2 PEOPLE EVERYWHERE

How wonderful it is,
Lord Jesus,
that people everywhere love you:
– people in big, big countries,
– and people on tiny, tiny islands.
Amen.

3 HE'S GOT THE WHOLE WORLD

Thank you, Lord Jesus,
    for making the whole world.
Thank you that everything is under your control,
    and we can trust you each day.
Amen.

4 ALL AGES

Dear Lord Jesus,
thank you for all the people
    who love you:
    – for the babies,
    – for the toddlers,
    – for the school children,
    – for the teenagers,
    – for the adults,
    – for the very old people.
Lord Jesus, so many people love you!
Amen.

5 EVERY COUNTRY

Dear Lord Jesus, thank you,
for your great love.
Thank you for loving everyone,
in every country,
all around the world.
Amen.

6 EVERY TYPE OF CHILD

Lord Jesus, you care for
    all different types of children:
    – noisy children,
    – quiet children,
    – clever children,
    – and children who are good
        at sports.
Help me to love everyone as well.
Amen.

7 A PRAYER FOR PEACE

Dear Lord Jesus,
you promised
your peace
to your first followers.
May I have your peace
in my life today,
and so spread peace
to everyone
I meet and talk to.
Amen.

8 SO DIFFERENT

Dear Lord Jesus, thank you
for making all the people
in the world so different
from each other.
Thank you for all the different languages,
all the different foods,
all the different ways of living,
all the different kinds of faces.
Thank you, Lord Jesus,
for the wonderful variety in your world.
Amen.

10 BEGIN WITH ME

Lord,
change the world –
and begin with me.
Amen.

11 MISSIONARIES

Thank you, Lord Jesus,
for people who have gone
to other countries
to tell others about you.
Please help them when their work is tough.
Please support them when people laugh at them.
Please encourage them when they feel like
giving up.
Amen.

12 WARS

Dear Lord God,
There are so many wars all over the world.
Please help people to stop hating and killing.
Help them to listen to each other,
to understand each other's problems,
and to work for peace.
Amen.

9 OUR WORLD

Thank you, Lord Jesus,
for making our wonderful world.
Please help us to care for your world,
for the animals, for the trees,
for the fish, and for the birds.
And please help us to love
the people in your world.
Amen.

People who need help

1 NO ONE TO LOVE THEM

Dear Father,
I pray for those who have no one
to love them enough to pray for them.
Wherever they are,
whoever they are,
let them know that they are not forgotten,
Amen.

St. Francis of Assisi

2 HUNGRY CHILDREN

Dear Lord Jesus,
please may hungry children
have enough food tonight;
please may thirsty children
have a drink tonight;
please may homeless children
have a home tonight.
Amen.

3 DISABLED PEOPLE

Dear Lord Jesus, you made
blind people see,
lame people walk,
and deaf people hear.
Please help all the people today who can't
see or hear or move about. Give them
patience, and peace, and trust in you.
And help me to understand how hard it is
to be disabled.
Amen.

4 SCHOOL TEACHERS

Thank you, Lord Jesus,
for all our school teachers.
Please give them lots of patience
and lots of good ideas
as they teach us.
Amen.

5 THE LONELY

Dear Lord Jesus, we thank you
for promising never to leave us.
Please may lonely people
know that you are with them.
Amen.

6 PEOPLE AT WORK

Dear Lord, we pray for all the people
   who work in towns and help to keep
   them going:
   – postmen and postwomen,
   – policemen and policewomen,
   – bus drivers and train drivers,
   – firemen and firewomen,
   – and supermarket staff.
Thank you for all the people who work so
   hard so we can enjoy each day.
Amen.

7 HEALERS

Thank you, Lord Jesus,
   for all people who are healers;
   – all doctors and nurses,
   – everybody who works in hospitals,
   – and for all people who find
     new medicines and cures.
Please make them wise and loving.
Amen.

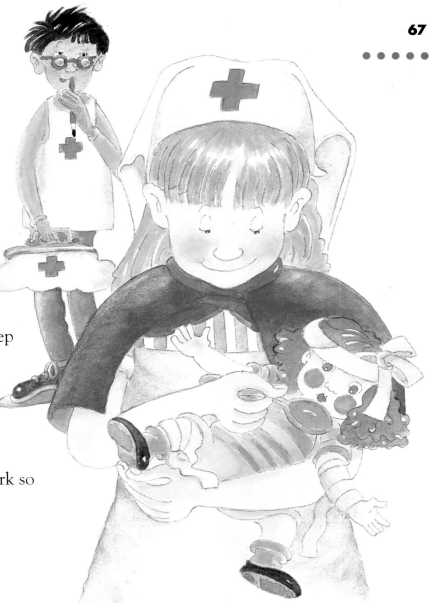

8 SICK PEOPLE

Care for your sick people,
   dear Lord Jesus.
Rest your tired people,
   dear Lord Jesus.
Comfort your dying people,
   dear Lord Jesus.
Amen.

St. Augustine

9 REFUGEES

Dear Lord Jesus, when you were a baby,
　your parents were refugees.
When you were a grown-up, you had no
　home of your own.
Dear Lord Jesus, be with all refugees and
　homeless people today. Help them to
　find homes of their own.
And be with all people working to help
　homeless people and refugees.
Amen.

10 THE WEAK AND WEARY

We bring before you, Lord God,
the troubles of people and nations:
　　– the sighing of prisoners,
　　– the sorrows of the bereaved,
　　– the helplessness of the weak,
　　– the feebleness of the old.
Lord God, be close to each of them.
Amen.

St. Anselm

11 FOR JUSTICE

Heavenly Father,
please be with all rulers, all judges
　in courts of law, all juries, all lawyers,
　and all the people who make laws.
Please help them to make wise and fair
　laws, and to make good decisions.
Amen.

12 PERSECUTED PEOPLE

Lord Jesus, we pray for people
who are in prison in some countries
just because they believe in you.
Please comfort them in prison.
Help organizations that work to free
people who are in prison for standing up
for what is right and true.
Amen.

Telling others

1 WE MUST SHINE

Jesus tells us, "Shine"
    With a pure, clear light;
Like a little candle
    Burning in the night.
In this world of darkness
    We must all shine –
You in your small corner,
    And I in mine.

Susan Warner

2 SHINING FOR JESUS

Jesus tells us, "Shine"
    First of all for him.
He will see and know it
    If our light grows dim.
He looks down from heaven
    To see us shine –
You in your small corner
    And I in mine.

Susan Warner

3 SHINE FOR ALL AROUND

Jesus tells us, "Shine"
    For all those around.
Many kinds of darkness
    In this world abound,
Sin and wars and sorrow –
    So we must shine.
You in your small corner
    And I in mine.

Susan Warner

4 LIPS THAT WE MIGHT TELL

He gave us eyes to see
    And lips that we might tell,
How great is God almighty,
    Who has made all things well.

C.F. Alexander

5 A LIFE TO TELL

Almighty God,
give us eyes to see you,
a heart to think about you,
and a life to tell others about you.
Amen.

St. Benedict

6 WE WILL TELL THE WORLD

We give thanks to you, Lord God,
We will tell the world how wonderful you
are.
We will tell the world about the
wonderful things you have done.

Psalm 75

7 TAKE MY VOICE

Take my voice, and let me sing
Always, only, for my King.
Take my lips and let them be
Filled with messages from
thee.

F.R. Havergal

8 FILL MY LIFE

Please fill my life, O Lord my God,
In every part with praise,
That my whole being may proclaim,
Your being and your ways.

H. Bonar

9 TO HELP OTHERS

Dear Lord Jesus,
help us
to help others,
to know you,
and to know your love.
Amen.

10 TO SHOW LOVE

Dear Lord Jesus,
help me to show your love
to everyone I meet today.
Amen.

11 ATTEMPT GREAT THINGS

Lord God,
help me to attempt great things for you,
and to expect great things from you.
Amen.

William Carey

12 OPEN MY LIPS

Dear Lord, open my lips
and my mouth will speak about you
Amen.

Psalm 51:15

Through the year

1 NEW YEAR

For the year that's past,
thank you, Lord Jesus.
For the year ahead,
I trust you, Lord Jesus.
Amen.

2 FEBRUARY DAYS

Icy winds,
    noses glow.
Frozen puddles,
    falling snow.
Spring a'waiting,
    snowdrops grow.
Thank you for February days.

3 MARCH: LENT

Dear Jesus,
for forty days you were alone in the desert
    with the wild animals. Help me to say
    no to wrong thoughts, just as you did.
Amen.

4 APRIL: EASTER

Dear Lord Jesus,
    how we love to celebrate
    Easter each April!
You are alive and with us each day.
Thank you, living Lord.
Amen.

5 MAY

Dear Creator God,
  you made everything.
Thank you for the delicate,
  full blossoms
  of the month of May.
Amen.

6 JUNE

So many people
are taking exams and tests.
Help them, Lord Jesus, to be quiet in
their own minds, to do their best,
and to trust you to bring about
your plans for them.
Amen.

7 JULY

Blazing sun,
  buzzing bees,
butterflies,
  shady trees,
flower-filled fields,
  and iced teas.
Thank you, Lord Jesus, for July days.
Amen.

8 AUGUST: HOLIDAYS

Dear Lord Jesus,
when your friends were tired
you took them away to a quiet place,
  by the lake, for a rest.
Thank you for our holidays.
Amen.

9 SEPTEMBER: HARVEST

We plow the fields and scatter
The good seed on the land,
But it is fed and watered
By God's almighty hand.
He sends the snow in winter,
The warmth to swell the grain,
The breezes and the sunshine,
And soft refreshing rain.

Chorus:
All good gifts around us
Are sent from heaven above.
So thank the Lord, O thank the Lord,
For all his love.

M. Claudius

10 OCTOBER: HALLOWEEN

Thank you, Lord Jesus, that everyone who
    trusts in you is kept safe from all evil –
    in this world and the next.
Amen.

11 NOVEMBER

For all your followers, Lord Jesus,
who now live with you in heaven,
we thank you for their courage,
their faithfulness,
and their love for you.
Amen.

12 DECEMBER

As we look forward
to Christmas time, Lord Jesus,
help us to remember
that we are celebrating your birthday.
Help us to remember
everything that you have given us
all through the year.
Amen.

Traveling on

1 CHRIST BESIDE ME

Christ be with me, Christ within me.
Christ behind me, Christ before me.
Christ beside me, Christ to win me.
Christ to comfort me, and restore me.
Christ beneath me, Christ above me.
Christ to quiet me, Christ in danger.
Christ in hearts of all that love me.
Christ in mouth of friend and stranger.

C.F. Alexander

2 NEVER LEAVE ME

Never leave me, nor forsake me,
   Always be my friend.
I need you from life's beginning,
   To its end.

W.J. Mathams

3 ALL OUR MOMENTS

Lord Jesus, always with us stay,
Make all our moments calm and bright,
Chase the dark night of sin away,
Spread through the world your holy light.

Roy Palmer

4 HAND IN HAND WITH JESUS

Dear Lord Jesus,
we put our hands
in your hand,
as we travel
with you
each day.

St. Augustine

5 IN A BOAT

Dear Lord, when we travel by boat
over waves on the sea,
be with us and keep us safe.

6 LEAD ME

Father, lead me, day by day,
Always in your own sweet way.
Teach me to be pure and true,
Show me what I ought to do.
Amen.

J.P. Hopps

7 DAY BY DAY

Day by day, dear Lord,
of you three things I pray –
to know you more clearly,
to love you more dearly,
to follow you more nearly,
day by day.
Amen.

Richard of Chichester

8 MY SHEPHERD

The king of love my shepherd is,
  Whose goodness fails me never.
I nothing lack if I am his
  And he is mine forever.

H.W. Baker

12 FOR BIKES AND TRUCKS

For bikes and trucks and trains,
For buses and for planes,
For barges, yachts, and boats,
For everything that floats,
For rockets that fly to the stars,
For tractors and for cars,
Thank you, Lord.
Help travelers stay safe,
obey the rules, and not get angry.
Amen.

9 GOD'S PATH

Dear heavenly Father, help me each day
  to choose the right way,
to reject wrong ways,
  to follow good ways,
  and always go your way.
Amen.

10 COMFORT

Dear Lord Jesus,
  as I get older,
  some things frighten me more and more.
Please stay next to me
  throughout all my life.
Amen.

11 JOURNEYS

Please keep us safe as we travel today, Lord
  Jesus.
Thank you for the excitement of getting
  ready for a journey.
Help us to remember that you come with us
  as we go.
Please bring us back home, safe and well.
Amen.

God make you happy

1 GOD BLESS YOU

God bless all those that I love,
God bless all those that love me.
God bless all those that love those
   that I love,
And all those that love those that love me.
Amen.

2 MAY THE LORD BLESS YOU

May the Lord bless us and take care of us:
May the Lord be kind and gracious to us:
May the Lord look on us with his favour
   and give us his peace.
Amen.

     Numbers 6:24-26

4 PRAISE GOD

Praise God, from whom all blessings flow;
   Praise him, all creatures here below;
Praise him above, you heavenly host –
   Praise Father, Son and Holy Ghost.

Thomas Ken

3 THE LOVE OF JESUS

May the love of the Lord Jesus
   draw us to himself.
May the power of the Lord Jesus
   strengthen us for his service.
May the joy of the Lord Jesus
   fill our lives.
Amen.

    William Temple

5 THE LORD BLESS YOU

The Lord bless you and keep you.
The Lord go with you
   to inspire and protect you.
The Lord open your ears to listen,
The Lord open your eyes to see,
The Lord open your heart
   to give and receive.
Amen.

6 IN THE PALM OF HIS HAND

May the road rise to meet you,
May the wind be always at your back,
May the sun shine warm on your face,
The rain fall softly on your fields.
May God hold you
   in the palm of his hand.
Amen.

7 THE FRIENDSHIP OF THE HOLY SPIRIT

May the grace of our Lord Jesus Christ,
the love of God,
and the friendship of the Holy Spirit,
be with us all.
Amen.

2 Corinthians 13

8 THE PEACE OF GOD

The peace of God,
which is beyond all understanding,
keep our hearts and minds
in the knowledge and love of God,
and of his Son,
Jesus Christ our Lord.
Amen.

Philippians 4:7

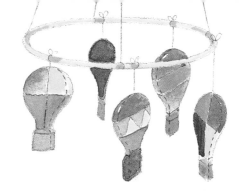

9 BLESS AND KEEP US

May the eternal God
bless us and keep us,
protect our bodies,
save our souls,
direct our thoughts,
and bring us safely
to our home with Jesus,
to live with him forever.
Amen.

12 PEACE

The peace of God be with us.
The peace of Christ be with us.
The peace of the Holy Spirit be with us
today, and every day of our lives.
Amen.

10 GOD SHINING ON US

May God be kind to us.
May God bless us.
May God make his face to shine on us.
Amen.

Psalm 67:1

11 BE NEAR, LORD JESUS

The Lord Jesus Christ
Be near to defend us,
Be within to refresh us,
Be around to preserve us,
Be in front to guide us,
Be behind to forgive us.
Amen.

Heaven

1 BEING WITH JESUS

Dear Lord Jesus, thinking about you
makes me feel so happy.
Thank you, for surrounding me
with your love, all the time.
Amen.

2 MEETING IN HEAVEN

Dear Lord Jesus,
we look forward
to meeting up with you
and all your followers
in heaven.

3 BEING WITH GOD

Dear Father God,
thank you for promising
that all your friends
will be in heaven
with you and with Jesus
after this life.
Amen.

4 LIVING FOREVER

Thank you, Lord Jesus,
that you have already prepared a place
in heaven for each of us who trust you.
Please help everyone in the world
to know that they can live with you
forever and ever.
Amen.

5 WITH JESUS, FOREVER

Dear Lord Jesus,
    you have told us that
    one day you will come again
    as a great king
    with your angels.
We can't wait to be with you,
    and with everyone who loves you,
    all together, forever.
Amen.

6 ALL OF GOD'S PEOPLE

Dear heavenly Father,
thank you that in heaven
we will be with you,
and we'll meet up with your other friends,
like Daniel, David, and Joseph.
Amen.

7 ALL OF JESUS' FOLLOWERS

Dear Lord Jesus,
thank you for being my special friend.
And thank you that we will see
all your other friends in heaven;
Like John, Peter, Mary and Paul.
Amen.

8 A NEW HEAVEN

Dear Lord Jesus, we are so looking forward
    to being with you in heaven.
Thank you for telling us
    that in heaven there is:
    – no more crying,
    – no more pain,
    – no more dying,
    – and no more sadness.
All these things will be gone.
Amen.

Revelation 21:1, 4

9 PREPARING A PLACE

Lord Jesus, you have told us
that you are preparing a place for us
  in heaven.
Prepare us also for that happy time,
so that where you are,
we may be with you always.
Amen.

William Penn

10 BRING US ALL HOME

Thank you,
Lord Jesus,
that we are with you now,
and that you are
bringing us home
to be with you in heaven.
Amen.

11 THE FORGIVEN THIEF

Dear Lord Jesus,
thank you for saying
to the thief
who trusted in you on the cross,
"Today you will be with me in paradise."
Amen.

Luke 23:43

12 LIKE JESUS' FOLLOWERS

Lord Jesus, thank you that heaven
is such a wonderful place,
where all your followers who have died
now sing your praises.
Amen.

9 A BIG THANK YOU

Almighty God,
Father of all mercies,
we your unworthy servants
do give you most humble and hearty
    thanks
for all your goodness
and loving-kindness to us,
and to all people.
Amen.

Bishop Reynolds

10 FOR ALL THE BLESSINGS

We thank you for
our creation,
preservation,
and all the blessings of this life.
But above all,
thank you for your overflowing love
in the redemption of the world
by our Lord Jesus Christ,
for the means of grace,
and for the hope of glory.
Amen.

Bishop Reynolds

11 THE JESUS PRAYER

Lord Jesus Christ,
Son of God,
have mercy on me,
a sinner.
Amen.

12 GOD BLESS US

God bless us
one and all.

Charles Dickens

Prayers from the Bible

1 I WILL PRAISE YOU

I will praise your greatness,
 my God and king.
I will praise your name for ever and ever.
Every day I will praise you.
I will speak about your greatness for ever
 and ever.
The Lord is great and worthy of being
 highly praised.
His greatness no one can understand.

Psalm 145:1-3

2 GIVE THANKS

Give thanks to the Lord,
because he is good.
His love goes on forever.
Amen.

Psalm 107:1

3 A PRAYER SUNG IN HEAVEN

Our Lord and God!
You are worthy to receive
glory, honor, and power.
For you created all things,
and by your will
they were given existence
and life.
Amen.

Revelation 4:11

4 DAVID'S PRAYER

The Lord is my light and my salvation,
No one can frighten me.
The Lord protects me from all danger,
I will never be afraid.

Psalm 27:1

5 SOLOMON'S PRAYER

Yours, Lord, is the greatness,
the power, the glory,
the splendor, and the majesty;
for everything in heaven and
 on earth is yours.
All things come from you,
and of your own do we give you.
Amen.

1 Chronicles 29:11-14

6 I LOVE YOU, O LORD

I love you, O Lord, my strength.
The Lord is my rock.
The Lord is my fortress.
The Lord is my deliverer.
My God is my rock
 who keeps me totally safe.
Amen.

Psalm 18:1-2

7 GUIDE ME

Guide me in your truth
 and teach me,
for you are my God and Savior.
My hope is in you
all the day long.
Amen.

Psalm 25

8 A PRAYER FOR JESUS' RETURN

Come, Lord Jesus.
Amen.

Revelation 22:20

9 A FATHER'S PRAYER FOR HIS ILL SON

Lord, I believe.
Help me to overcome my unbelief.
Amen.

Mark 9:24

10 PAUL PRAYS FOR HIS FRIENDS

I pray that you and all God's holy people will
have the power to understand the
greatness of Christ's love.
I pray that you can understand
how wide and
how long and
how high and
how deep
that love is.
Amen.

Ephesians 3:18, International Children's Bible

11 FOR CHRISTIANS IN ROME

May the God of hope
fill you
with all joy and peace
as you trust in him,
so that you may overflow
with hope
by the power
of the Holy Spirit.
Amen.

Romans 15:13

12 PEACE AT ALL TIMES

May the Lord of peace himself
give you peace
at all times
and in every way.
The Lord be with you all.

St. Paul in 2 Thessalonians 3:16

Prayers Jesus prayed

1 **THANK YOU, FATHER**

I thank you,
Father,
that you listen to me.
I know that you
always hear me.

John 11:41-42

2 **ORDINARY PEOPLE**

My Father, Lord of heaven and earth,
I am grateful that you hid all this
from wise and educated people
and showed it to ordinary people.
Yes, Father, that is what pleased you.

Luke 10:21

3 **TROUBLE**

Now my heart
is troubled.
Father,
bring glory
to your name.

John 12:27-28

4 **MY DISCIPLES**

Father,
my prayer is not
that you take them
out of the world
but that you protect them
from the evil one.

John 17:15

5 UNITED IN JESUS

I pray that they may all be one.
Father!
May they be in us,
just as you are in me
and I am in you.

John 17:21, Good News Bible

6 GIVE GLORY

Father,
the hour has come.
Give glory to your Son,
so that the Son
may give glory to you.

John 17:1, Good News Bible

7 BEFORE JESUS WAS ARRESTED

Father,
if it is your will,
take this cup of suffering
away from me.
Not my will, however,
but your will be done.

Luke 22:42, Good News Bible

8 WITH ME

Father!
You have given your followers to me,
and I want them to be with me
where I am,
so that they may see my glory.

John 17:24, Good News Bible

9 FORGIVE THEM

Father,
forgive them.
For they do not know
what they are doing.

Luke 23:34

10 FROM THE CROSS

My God,
my God,
why did you abandon me?

Matthew 27:46, Good News Bible

11 A CRY OF VICTORY

It is finished.

John 19:30

12 I PLACE MY SPIRIT

Father!
In your hands
I place my spirit!

Luke 23:46, Good News Bible

Goodnight

1 GUARD US

Save us, dear Lord,
while waking,
and guard us while sleeping,
that awake we may watch with Christ
and asleep we may rest in peace.
Amen.

2 LOVING SHEPHERD

Loving Shepherd of your sheep,
   May your lamb in safety sleep.
Let your angels round me stand,
   None can take me from your hand.

J.E. Leeson

3 WHILE WE SLEEP

Before the ending of the day,
Creator of the world, we pray,
that you with your constant care
   would keep
Your watch around us as we sleep.
Amen.

4 GOD BLESS

The moon shines bright,
The stars give light.
God bless us all,
Both great and small.

5 WATCH, DEAR LORD

Watch, dear Lord,
with those who wake,
or watch,
or weep tonight,
And give your angels charge
over those who sleep.
Amen.

St. Augustine

6 A QUIET NIGHT

The Lord Almighty
grant us a quiet night
and a perfect end.
Amen.

7 LIGHTEN OUR DARKNESS

Lighten our darkness,
Lord, we pray;
and in your great mercy
defend us
from all dangers of this night
for the love of your only Son,
our Savior, Jesus Christ. Amen.

The Book of Common Prayer

8 KEEP ME SAFE

Lord, keep me safe this night
and take away my fears.
May angels guard me while I sleep,
till morning light appears.

Traditional

9 SLEEP IN PEACE

In peace I will lie down and sleep,
For you alone, Lord,
Keep me perfectly safe.
Amen.

Psalm 4:8

10 LITTLE CHILDREN

Lord, when there is not any light
And mom and dad are asleep,
Then, through the stillness
    of the night
Your little children keep.
Amen.

A. Matheson

12 PRAISE AND REST

The day you gave us, Lord, is ending
    thank you for all I did (especially _____).
Help me to rest now
    and wake up all refreshed in
        the morning.
Amen.

11 FUN AND REST

Thank you, Lord Jesus,
for all the fun we have had today.
Thank you, Lord Jesus,
for all the rest we'll enjoy tonight.
Amen.

Index
to the first line of the prayers